20

Life Lessons

FOR YOUR THIRTIES

Farima Wassel Joya

7 Treasures
PRESS

Printed in the United States

20 Life Lesson Series, Vol 2
20 Life Lessons for your 30s
First Edition

By: Farima Wassel Joya

ISBN-13: 9780998661100 (7 Treasures Press)
ISBN-10: 0998661104

Library of Congress Control Number:
2017901370

Published by 7 Treasures Press
www.7treasures.com
7tpress@7treasures.com
(510) 275-3497

To my daughter, Sahar Assifi

Introduction

Life is an interesting journey. As time passes by, you grow up without noticing anything different from day to day. You have the opportunity to become mature after passing through every obstacle that comes your way. Each obstacle teaches you a unique lesson that only you can experience and learn from. For the rest of your life, you will follow your knowledge and wisdom to go through your life's journey as an individual. From time to time, you will realize that what you have is not enough, and that is when reading and learning from other people's experiences comes in handy. People share their wisdom in the hopes of making a difference in other people's lives.

If you want to have no regrets in life, you will ask older and wiser people to share the best lessons they've learned so you can use them in your life. You may ask a question and get your answers, but due to your young age, you are not able to grasp the advice or don't know exactly how to apply it to your life. But when the time comes, you'll remember the lesson and will be able to apply it to your life naturally. Therefore, if you don't agree or cannot grasp a lesson, or don't yet feel ready to apply these lessons, you can wait as long as it takes. Sooner or later, you'll know how to ask the right questions, or even what to ask first, and you'll have the answers already in your mind. There's a famous quote that says, when a student is ready, the master appears. This could not be more true. At any age or stage of life you are in, you will have blind spots or gray areas that hold all your questions. When you are ready to ask questions, seek knowledge, solve a problem, or know what kind of questions to ask, the master appears and doors will open for you.

You've passed through your twenties and have obviously made some choices on how to begin your life's journey. Or, perhaps you were on an unintentional path heading in an undesired direction. Whatever the case may be, your twenties are gone, and you are still at the beginning of the next best decade of your life. You'll have many opportunities to make up for lost opportunities and/or grab new ones. I hope these humble twenty life lessons will help you move forward towards a life that is filled with your unique gifts to this universe. I only wish that you will utilize these lessons and find your own path of life with ease and joy.

Sharing Is Caring

I share these 20 life lessons with my daughter, Sahar Assifi. She has just begun her thirties, but her maturity level has always been higher than her age.

You, too, must understand that whoever shared the gift of this book with you loves you and cares about you. After reading it, please pass it on to someone who you love and care for a lot too.

Farewell to your youth;
it was good while it lasted!

Unknown

20 Life Lessons For Your 20s

Just in case you did not pick up a copy of 20 Life Lessons for Your Twenties, here is your chance. Some people are further along and some are behind with their age-related activities and maturity, but you can start from today and from wherever you are in life now. It's never too late to do the right thing.

1. Forget planning for the rest of your life
2. Make a vision board
3. Give your parents a reason to trust you
4. Detach from your old friends and make new ones
5. Develop a unique character trait
6. Take your finances seriously
7. Pick your role models but follow your heart
8. Be active
9. Plan a solo trip
10. Explore art
11. Don't get emotionally involved
12. Monitor your community, your country and the world
13. Avoid self-destructive behaviors
14. Admit you don't know
15. Say no to peer/parent pressure
16. Speak your mind
17. Trust your guts and take risks
18. Help people to help you

19. Find your passion
20. Be flexible and adaptable

Keep these lessons in mind and practice them if you are not already doing so. Now, are you ready for the most valuable life lessons for your thirties?

1

LIVE YOUR WAY

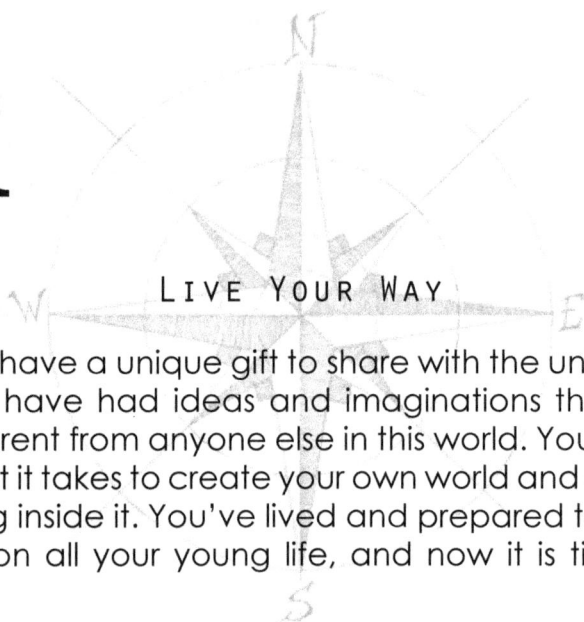

You have a unique gift to share with the universe. You have had ideas and imaginations that are different from anyone else in this world. You have what it takes to create your own world and everything inside it. You've lived and prepared to take action all your young life, and now it is time to act.

Your inspiration should come from your imagination; from everything that you have dreamed of up until now to make it happen for yourself. With your actions and decisions, you sometimes hit the target, and sometimes you make mistakes. This is a fact of life, and there are consequences for your actions, but the burden of making a wrong decision keeps many from making any decision at all, and that is a big mistake in life. Mistakes and failure should not hold you back from trying again and again. They're your best springboard to living your life while being true to yourself.

The greatest risk in life is not taking risks to do it your way without any kind of fear. Your ideas, dreams and goals are real, and now is the time to make an action plan to turn them into a reality.

If you ask, "What if my husband (or my wife) doesn't let me do things my way?" there's a very simple solution to that: Negotiate. Give a little to gain a little. It is very natural, and almost every couple faces similar control situations. However, in healthy and happy relationships couples support and trust each other to enjoy life without judgment. So, give time and space to your spouse to do the things he/she loves to do, and ask the same in return.

You might not get 100 percent your way all the time, but it will be close enough to give you the satisfaction of living your unique life your way.

2

FORGET YOUR CHILDHOOD

You have begun your own journey; you are an adult and can make all your own decisions. Whether you had a fairy-tale childhood or not, that is all in the past. You cannot make your future decisions based on your childhood experiences. You did not have any control over how you were raised. That part of your life belonged to your parents or your caretakers, and was influenced by their lifestyle. It is unnecessary to bring the baggage of your childhood into your present and future life.

Now, it is your time. You make the rules, and you have all the options. If you had a bad childhood, you'll need to forgive your caretakers and move on with a clean slate. If you had a fairy-tale childhood where you were not in touch with the reality of life, you will also need to learn some hard lessons and adjust yourself to your current reality. Instead of feeling frustrated or like a failure, you'll need to forgive your parents and give yourself a chance of a clean start.

If you ever did things to please others - your parents, your family, your teachers, or your bosses - now is the time to stop. Pleasing others does not serve you any longer because you will not be able to please everyone all the time. It takes much time and effort for nothing. Practice saying NO politely, without hurting anyone's feelings.

The point is to look forward and move on. Think of yourself in five, ten, or even twenty years from now. You can make a difference in your life even if you start from this moment on. Today is the beginning of the rest of your life.

3

YOUR FAMILY IS YOUR PRIORITY

Now that you are at the beginning of your real life-building stage, you either have a family already, or you will have one very soon. Just as you are learning to live your way with a clean, fresh, and positive foot forward, you should realize that your family is your top priority. You are sharing your life with your spouse and your children, and it literally means sharing your life. The lives of your spouse and children depend on you. They look up to you for emotional, physical, financial, and social support. You will have to provide for them, as much as you can, with love and care. Remember that you will either make good or bad memories for your children when they are grown up, so the choice is obvious. When making your family life's decisions, you can ask for advice, but never give an opportunity to anyone to intrude, clutter your judgment, or make decisions for you. You'll need to trust your heart and make some family decisions from it.

Your parents, siblings, aunts, uncles, and cousins are your support group. Their role is very important in your life, but in most cases, their livelihood does not depend on you. Simply not realizing this fact breaks apart so many families. This is the only secret to building and maintaining a happy and healthy family.

Your actions speak much louder to your own family. You are your kids' role model, and you are their first teacher. Do more of the things you want to see more of in your family, and less of the things that you don't want to see or experience. You are a mirror reflecting your kids' future. As such, the choice of how you run your life is with you.

4

HAVE A HOBBY & A SUNCTURARY

You have the huge responsibility of providing for your family, working, building your career, and dealing with your kids' chores. These are very important things that can take up all of your attention, energy, and time. And, we know that life is a moving journey. One hurdle after another will appear and will keep you busy every minute of your day and night. So, in order to function as a healthy and happy person you need to schedule a slot of regular time off for yourself to refresh and gather your energy and refocus. It is best to have a hobby; something to boost your imagination and keep you preoccupied. You can play a musical instrument, or just listen to music, meditate, practice yoga, read a light or funny book, sew, knit, cook, bake, paint, or write. A fifteen-minute nap in the middle of the day or meditation in a quiet place is very necessary to keep you a sane, loving, productive and functional person.

Have a comfortable space in any part of your home that you can call your sanctuary. Decorate it with your colors and your style. It should give you the needed comfort at any given time without leaving your home. This is a place in which to meditate, to drink a cup of tea, to think, to listen to music, to do an activity that you enjoy the most.

Outside of your home, have a few places in your city like your sanctuary at home where you can drink a cup of coffee, read a book, write a journal, have lunch with friends, or be in nature.

The more you use these mini sanctuary trips, the more you'll enjoy life and everyone around you. Make it happen!

5

HAVE A FINANCIAL PLAN

This is probably a time when you have a steady job and income. Start by putting a small amount of money away from every paycheck for emergencies and for the unknowns. The goal is to have at least six months of your expenses stashed away; anything above that amount should be invested in an income-producing asset.

However, never go overboard with stashing money away in the hopes of permanent financial security because you don't know what tomorrow will bring you. Spend your money within your budget and means now, because the experiences and enjoyments that you can have at this moment are so much better than ten years from now. Life is now!

Just to be safe and have your peace of mind, invest in life insurance for yourself and your family once you have children. This account can be set up with a set amount of monthly payments that will never increase.

It is also not too early to think of investing in a small retirement account because the little investment that you can make at an early age will be re-invested with compound interest annually and will grow to a significant amount of money for your retirement years. Small and steady investment into a retirement account as early as possible will give you the greatest reward. You can use the benefits of early withdrawal for emergencies, or you can invest your retirement savings into other income-producing, tax-deferred investment accounts like real estate and stocks.

6

BUY YOUR FIRST HOME

Home ownership should be the first asset in your financial portfolio. Not only will you benefit from providing a stable life for your family, but you will also reap considerable financial rewards.

The best part of buying a house is that you don't need the full amount of the home you are buying. You can get financing for up to 95 percent of the price, which you will pay monthly. However, you will have the reward of ownership from the time you sign the contract and get the keys to your first home.

With home ownership you save on taxes annually by deducting the mortgage interest from your taxable income; the value of your home appreciates regularly and you build equity by living in your own home.

If you like the process, you can start investing in real estate as a side business or a full-time career.

It can be a very profitable and rewarding

business. Buy and sell your own home every few years for profit before investing. This is an area to do more research in, and contact people with similar careers to learn more about investing in real estate as a career.

7

CHANGE CAREERS

Although it is very tough for you and your family to go through a career change at this time, if you are not happy with what you do now, it will be that way for many years to come. In the end, you will cause more pain and unhappiness to yourself and your family members by not changing your career. When you do something that you like, everyone will be happy and it will be worth the short-term sacrifice and hardship to go through the change. However, you will need to be sure of the change. Is the new career really as attractive as it appears from outside? You can always start as an intern, or with a part-time job, or at least interview people in the field to know all the pros and cons of your career change. Just make sure you are passionate about what you do and you'll be happy doing it.

Before changing careers, you need to look at the numerous possibilities and different angles of your current career and identify the many ways in which you can solve problems and how best you can do it. Narrow down your options and stay with it.

Become an expert and specialize in one thing. With a small and narrow but deep niche, you'll go far with work satisfaction, recognition, and producing income.

8

VOLUNTEER

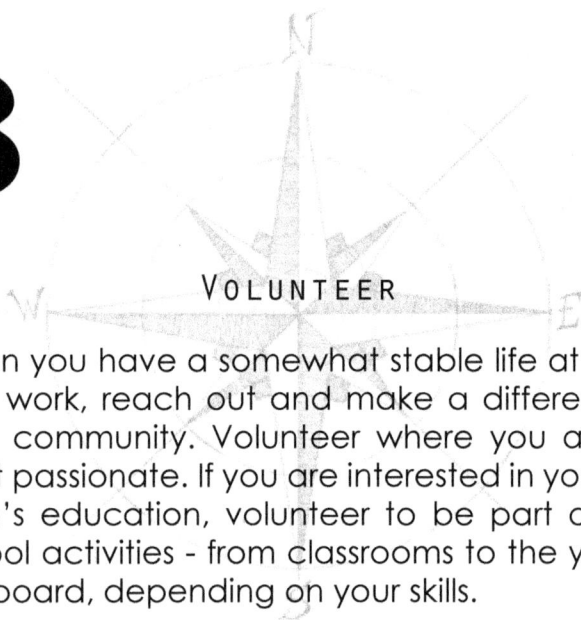

When you have a somewhat stable life at home and work, reach out and make a difference in your community. Volunteer where you are the most passionate. If you are interested in your children's education, volunteer to be part of their school activities - from classrooms to the yard to the board, depending on your skills.

You will get the reward of being connected with people in the same area for the same cause. That will bring you new opportunities and new ideas to explore.

Volunteering is valuable work that will teach your children to do the same: to care about community projects, team activities, and how to be involved in making decisions outside of your control and home.

We all know that the needs of some people cannot and will not be met by the government agencies alone. The need is great if we look around. Seniors, young children, sick, disabled and poor. Some might need temporary help and some might be in need of longer-term care by people just like you to volunteer out of their goodwill and humanity.

Research has shown that when you care for others, you actually do more for yourself. Here are some of those benefits:

- Connects you to others. You'll make new friends and strengthen existing friendships.

- Increases social and relationship skills.

- Reduces your stress, anxiety and anger; combats depression, boosts self-confidence, and helps you stay physically active.

- Teaches you career experiences and helps you gain valuable job skills.

- Brings fun and fulfillment to your life.

9

Go On Vacation

Take at least one long vacation and many short ones annually. Your vacation does not need to be far or expensive. It can be to your neighborhood campground, or visiting somewhere where the value of the currency is less. Long vacations energize and refuel you for the rest of the year. You will have priceless memories from your vacations.

Vacationing will save you and your family from depression, being bored, unhappiness, and the routine duties of home, school, and work.

Your children will only remember the happy days with you when they grow up. So, provide them with as many opportunities to have good childhood memories as you can.

Vacation increases your physical and mental power to produce more, stay healthy, and focus better. Burnout is one of the main reasons for loss of productivity, mental breakdowns, being tired and uninterested. Break the routine because routine and doing the same thing over and over is the road to insanity.

Life is about doing and experiencing new things, new places, new people, new food, and new activities. Do it with your family and friends, because nothing helps in strengthening relationships more than going on a fun vacation together.

Plan your vacations way in advance because just the thought of going on vacation soon is enjoyable.

10

TIME WITH FAMILY & FRIENDS

Family members or whoever you call family are your support or your circle of influence. You give and receive and share good and bad times together. The goal is to share happy times with people you love and care for. Watch movies, go to the park for a picnic, swim, play ball, walk, fish, and have fun together. Stay away from people who are unhappy, gossipy, negative, and demanding. Dramatic people create stress and unhappiness.

Good friends and family members are needed around you to share good and bad times together. You laugh and cry with them. Share as much as you can, give as much as you can, and be open to receiving at the same time. Your family, especially your kids, will benefit the most from interactions with different people around them. They will build up happy and good memories around those people and learn how to make connections when they are older.

Your ultimate happiness and peace of mind in life comes from sharing time with likeminded people.

It is also very important to be available to your friends and family. Just as you count on them, you also should have their loyal connections. It's a matter of integrity and trust, which you will need to build over time.

11

HAVE AN OPEN MIND

Broaden your horizon about cultures and cuisines. Read books, watch documentaries, and get interested in international issues. Your life is not one-dimensional; it is all connected to your environment, plants, animals, and of course, other human beings. You are a unique individual, yet interconnected with your environment. As such, you need to learn about other cultures, belief systems, lifestyles, rituals, clothing styles, history, geography, and politics. You will be much happier if you can be open minded and accepting of anything that is different from you. When you notice how the world is interconnected and everything is dependent on everything else for survival, you will refrain from any type of prejudice and exclusivity.

Become friends with someone from a different culture or visit a country and look for similarities rather than differences. Learn about their communal lifestyle, language, and food so you can teach your children about them. Open your doors and your heart to people who are less fortunate; help out with their causes and create an atmosphere of living in harmony with all.

There's always two sides to any story; big or small. You might see one side clearly, but the other side is not known to you, so don't make any judgement about the truth of the matter until you are in the light of both sides of the story. This is not a simple thing to do, but open mindedness will help you to ask more questions about the truth of the other side before forming your own opinion on the story.

12

Venting Your Frustration

There will be a lot of times when you are frustrated and tired, and all you want to do is yell and show your frustration. Yelling, calling others names, cursing, using hurtful words, and being impatient all alienate family members, kill their self-esteem and self-confidence, and make them lose trust in each other. Come up with a method for getting frustration out along with your family members so everyone understands the situation and recognizes it when it comes up. You need to be a good role model for your children and show them patience by practice. They will do the same if and when they are frustrated.

Be patient and never give up on your children's struggles and issues, whether it is physical, mental, or social. They will need to solve their issues and overcome their struggles on their own with your support. Never jump to conclusions and/or solve their problems for them. It takes a lot on your part, but if you want to raise children who can take care of themselves at any stage of their lives, you'll be doing the right thing.

Your kids should always know that you love them unconditionally and will support them in any situation, even if they make mistakes.

Life can be tough for your kids as well. It is much better to have a set method for handling frustration in your family. At a time when someone is in a bad mood or has had a rough day, everyone knows what to do. Instead of your bad mood, or hurting others physically or emotionally, take a break away from everyone. Go to your room, breathe, and just go for a walk, and don't come back until you are feeling better. Your family deserves the peace and calmness that you want to provide them with. This method will save you from much unhappiness in the long run.

13

NEW RELATIONSHIP WITH PARENTS

Now that the control of building the relationship is with you, you will set your parents' role in your life. Your parents obviously want the best for you all the time; however, sometimes unconsciously they harm you and cause you more pain out of love. This is the time you set your priorities and treat them as friends who are involved with your life, but do not run it.

Grandparents have a very unique and special place in the life of their grandchildren. They might not have been good parents, but they would make good grandparents. However, you always can limit their boundaries and involvement for a mutually beneficial relationship with your children.

Your parents will always be a part of your life. If by chance your parents respect your rules and decisions and are part of your life without interfering, you can let them spoil your children.

On the other hand, your parents also should understand that they are not responsible for your mistakes, failures, and/or bad decisions. They did what they could and are done raising you. Now it is time for them to sit back and enjoy the fruit of their lives' investment.

14

EAT HEALTHY

Life can be tough and overwhelming for you, and you will undoubtedly be tempted to save time and buy ready-made food for yourself and your family. However, if you consider the value of good food that nourishes your body, you will never take this shortcut. Boxed meals, fast-food chains, big food and meat-processing companies are there for profit; they couldn't care less about the quality of food that you put in your body. Regardless of what the package label says, prepared meals are not good sources of nutrition.

It's your responsibility to keep your family happy and healthy, and a big part of that responsibility is providing healthy food for them. You need to educate yourself about the source of the food, even the fresh food, before you eat it.

If you can't grow your vegetables and raise your own meat, the best thing is to find local sources: farmers' markets, community gardens, and the organic corner of your grocery store are the places where you should be shopping for food. Eat only fresh, non-GMO, unprocessed food.

15

LEARN TO MEDITATE

If you are short on time and cannot do the things you love to do, or simply aren't enjoying everything you have, your home, and your work, then you need to step back and allow rejuvenation time in your day on a daily basis. Just like any good return on investment, your small investment in time for meditation will reap you great rewards.

As you start, it might take longer to stay in a meditative state, but it becomes easier with practice.

Meditation is a state between being awake and asleep. You are fully aware of your environment but in a complete empty zone. The goal is to be present and feel each organ of your body. Meditation is going inward for finding clarity and peace of mind. You will put a stop to your brain's activities and feel your body and real longing. Stay in this mood as often as possible and for as long as possible to rejuvenate your thoughts, focus on your inner wishes, and take a break from yourself.

Your meditation doesn't have to be long, and doesn't require a specific place, attire or atmosphere. Its only requirement is to close your eyes, go inward and feel your breath going in and out of your chest. You can do it while waiting in a doctor's office, standing in a line at the bank, lying down on your bed, a short break in between your drives in the car.

There are plenty of resources available to start your meditation practice today. Your personal, occupational, and social success depends on this lesson.

16

EXERCISE

Do you know that moving our body is the natural state of being for humans? Humans are supposed to walk and move, just like any other animal on this earth. However, over time, we have become lazier and lazier because of advancements bringing convenience to every aspect of the human life. Inventions did bring us convenience, but at the same time they've taken away a natural and important part of our ability to keep moving. Can you imagine how much more convenient your life is than a person who lived a thousand years before you? A hundred years before you? You cook your ready-made food on a convenient stovetop near your living room; you park your car a few steps from your house; you wash your clothes with the turn of two knobs; you can go to the other side of the earth in 12 hours; you wear ready-made clothes; you use disposable diapers for your kids; you can see and converse with someone anywhere on this earth instantly... you get the idea.

If you had the choice of growing your own food in your backyard, preparing and cooking fresh food, raising animals for your dairy and meat use, washing your own clothes with hands, getting your drinking water from a well, making a fire to keep the house warm or cook your food, and washing your dirty dishes in a stream, you would not need the gym.

Now that you have a convenient and comfortable life, you will need to move and keep moving in order to stay healthy to enjoy everything you have. After all, you have the opportunity to choose your favorite activity: swimming, biking, hiking, river rafting, running, tennis, basketball, baseball, soccer, or to do more than one of these activities. The goal is to move and keep moving every day.

Exercise pumps blood to your brain and muscles, and makes you feel good.

17

CLEAN YOUR CLUTTER

You are from a generation of games, computers, cell phones, packaged food, and reality TV shows, and most of you are living an unorganized and cluttered life. Now, real life and enjoying the simple things around you requires you to focus and to clean and unclutter your surroundings. This gives you a clear mind, space, reduces stress, and helps you to feel good both physically and mentally.

Keep things if you think you will need them next week, but never become a hoarder by keeping everything you think you might need one day. Clean out your closets and donate things you haven't used recently, or simply don't buy much stuff. Collecting stuff is a burden on your budget and space.

Very soon, you will realize that life is not about collecting stuff, gadgets and papers. It's about living comfortably with necessities.

Regular maintenance is the key to a stress-free life for you and your family.

A good rule of thumb is to throw away & give away two items for every new item you buy. Or have regular garage sales. Decluttering your home and space helps to clear your mind and sharpen your focus.

The other important point is to clean up after yourself right on the spot. If things are left to be done later, it'll pile up and become a disaster. The best practice is to just do it right there in the time and space that you are in. Practicing this habit is a great way to raise a healthy family in a healthy home.

18

BE PRESENT NOW

This is easier said than done. In order for you to enjoy the present moment now, you need to consciously choose to do so. Choose a moment that you'll enjoy, which could be any moment of your day. Your hot cup of tea or coffee, your healthy meal, a quiet moment of deep breathing, watching your kids laughing and playing, making someone happy, and many more moments in a day are great times to stop thinking about the past or the future and enjoy that moment.

Life happens now, and it's very important to enjoy what you have at the moment. It might not be an ideal place or activity, but you can still find a way to appreciate the better things in your life and be happy with wherever you are and whatever you are doing. You cannot postpone your present moment by thinking about the future. Chances are that the future won't happen the way you want it to happen, and in the process, you lose the present moment.

Be a little relaxed and forget to do everything by the book. It's the detour that brings excitement to life, and that is the art of living.

Living in the present moment takes a lot of conscious practice. The more you practice, the easier it gets.

19

STAY POSITIVE

Happiness is contagious. Even when things are not going well and you are not feeling your best, you still need to keep your positive energy and smile because this way you are not transmitting your sadness and negative energy to your family.

Unhappy situations arise in everyone's lives, but it's best to always know that it is only temporary and it will pass and you will overcome. Everyone falls repeatedly along the way of life's journey, but the ones who get up and continue are the ones who will succeed and live happier lives.

Of course, it's always okay to communicate your true feelings and be honest about bad or sad situations. Share your feelings with everyone so they know your state of mind and can better understand you, but try to keep your down moments to a minimum and do everything possible to change your feelings for a better tomorrow.

Just keep in mind that minor issues like being stuck in a traffic jam, or dealing with your boss's bad day, or not completing your projects as well as you had hoped are not reasons to prevent you from positive thinking and take away your good mood. Smile and everything will be different.

If you remember this little lesson, you will have many happier moments to remember in your life.

20

BE CURIOUS

Ask questions; don't believe things you see on the surface. Is it good for you or not? What's in it for you? What's the motive behind it? How will I or my family benefit from it? Is it necessary? How do I feel about it? How serious is it? Is it an opportunity or a fad?

We live in a world where people live for themselves and do everything possible to gain more of everything. This is not something new; it has always been the case. People who don't ask questions and are not curious can be victimized in every aspect of their lives. They can be taken advantage of at every opportunity. Ask questions of yourself, but don't judge other people for their actions or reactions because they have their own motives that might be totally different from yours.

Our world is now controlled by giant corporations in a capitalist society. Their number-one goal is to make a profit. They want you to believe they are on your side, but that is not the case. So, it is very important to know your rights and your facts before using any services or products. If something looks too good to be true, the chances are that it is.

You need to ask and find out the source of your food; you need to ask about the side effects of your medicines; you need to ask about the background or behind the scenes of your children's day care & school; you need to learn the motives of the books that your children read; and you need to know alternative ways of dealing with every issue in your life. Obviously, every service and product in the market has been created to benefit the creator that might not be beneficial to you. Find out what's in it for you, and what's in it for them. Sometimes, you need to give to receive; however, many times what you give is much greater than what you are receiving in return. Ask questions, and be curious.

About The Author

Born and raised in Afghanistan, Farima has gone through many obstacles to be where she is today. She lives on the Hawaiian Islands and enjoys a simple life. She is a multi-passionate author, publisher, and a practicing yogi on the path to self-discovery and higher spirituality.

Author of:

• How to Live Your Life with 7 Treasures You Own

• 20 Life Lessons Series

To get copies of these books and other books published by 7 Treasures Press, or to read her blogs on the Art of Living and find out more information, please visit www.7treasures.com.

7Treasures.com
7tpress@7treasures.com
510-275-3497
@7tpress